RAINFORESTS

Alexis Roumanis

LET'S READ
AV²
BY WEIGL™
ADDED VALUE • AUDIO VISUAL

Go to **www.av2books.com**, and enter this book's unique code.

BOOK CODE

L542838

AV² **by Weigl** brings you media enhanced books that support active learning.

AV² provides enriched content that supplements and complements this book. Weigl's AV² books strive to create inspired learning and engage young minds in a total learning experience.

Your AV² Media Enhanced books come alive with...

Audio
Listen to sections of the book read aloud.

Video
Watch informative video clips.

Embedded Weblinks
Gain additional information for research.

Try This!
Complete activities and hands-on experiments.

Key Words
Study vocabulary, and complete a matching word activity.

Quizzes
Test your knowledge.

Slide Show
View images and captions, and prepare a presentation.

... and much, much more!

Published by AV² by Weigl
350 5ᵗʰ Avenue, 59ᵗʰ Floor New York, NY 10118
Websites: www.av2books.com   www.weigl.com

Library of Congress Cataloging-in-Publication Data

Roumanis, Alexis.
 Rainforests / Alexis Roumanis.
    pages cm. -- (Exploring Ecosystems)
 Includes index.
 ISBN 978-1-4896-3018-6 (hard cover : alk. paper) -- ISBN 978-1-4896-3019-3 (soft cover : alk. paper) --
 ISBN 978-1-4896-3020-9 (single user ebook) -- ISBN 978-1-4896-3021-6 (multi-user ebook)
 1. Rain forest ecology--Juvenile literature. 2. Rain forests--Juvenile literature. I. Title.
 QH541.5.R27R68 2016
 577.34--dc23
                          2014044103

Printed in the United States of America in Brainerd, Minnesota
1 2 3 4 5 6 7 8 9 0 19 18 17 16 15

012015
WEP051214   Project Coordinator: Jared Siemens
                             Design: Mandy Christiansen

Weigl acknowledges iStock and Getty Images as the primary image suppliers for this title.

Contents

This is a rainforest.
A rainforest is a large, warm forest
where rain falls much of the time.

Some of the wettest places on Earth are rainforests. Most rainforests are found near Earth's equator.

The Amazon Rainforest in South America is the biggest rainforest in the world.

Most rainforests get more
than 70 inches
(178 centimeters) of
rainfall each year.

The Rafflesia is the world's
biggest flower. It grows in the
rainforests of Southeast Asia.

Morpho butterflies eat fallen fruit off the forest floor.

Agoutis are the only animals that can open Brazil nuts.

Capuchin monkeys spread pollen from tree to tree.

Toucans nest in holes found high up in trees.

A rainforest ecosystem is a place made up of animals and plants that need each other in order to live.

Orchids grow on the sides of trees so that they can be closer to sunlight.

Plants are an important part of a rainforest ecosystem. They provide food and shelter for the animals that live there.

Poinsettia plants often bloom in December.

The fruit of a Brazil nut tree is as big as a baseball.

Rubber tree sap is used to make car tires.

Chocolate is made from the beans of the cacao tree.

One banana plant can grow up to 150 bananas.

Many different animals
make their homes
in the rainforest.

Vampire bats
drink the
blood of
other animals.

Anacondas
are the largest
snakes on Earth.

The skin of the poison
dart frog helps keep it
safe from predators.

Rainforests are sometimes called the lungs of the planet. Their trees make much of the air people and animals need to breathe.

Nearly 400 billion trees live in the Amazon Rainforest.

Rainforests around the world are getting smaller every year. People cut down trees and sell them.

About 2,000 trees are cut down each minute in rainforests around the world.

People burn trees down in the rainforest to use the land for farms. These fires sometimes burn more rainforest than people mean to burn.

People can help save the rainforest by planting trees.

Rainforest Quiz

See what you have learned about rainforest ecosystems.

Find these rainforest animals and plants in the book. What are their names?

KEY WORDS

Research has shown that as much as 65 percent of all written material published in English is made up of 300 words. These 300 words cannot be taught using pictures or learned by sounding them out. They must be recognized by sight. This book contains 82 common sight words to help young readers improve their reading fluency and comprehension. This book also teaches young readers several important content words, such as proper nouns. These words are paired with pictures to aid in learning and improve understanding.

Page	Sight Words First Appearance
4	a, is, large, much, of, the, this, time, where
7	are, earth, found, in, most, near, on, places, some, world
8	each, get, grows, it, more, than, year
10	animals, can, eat, from, high, off, only, open, that, to, tree, up
11	and, be, live, made, need, other, plants, sides, so, they
12	an, as, big, food, for, important, often, part, there
13	car, make, one
14	group
15	different, helps, homes, keep, many, their
16	air, people, sometimes
19	about, around, cut, down, every, them
20	by, farms, land, mean, these, use

Page	Content Words First Appearance
4	forest, rain, rainforest
7	Amazon Rainforest, equator
8	flower, rainfall
10	agoutis, butterflies, floor, fruit, holes, monkeys, nuts, pollen, toucans
11	ecosystem, orchids, sunlight
12	baseball, December, shelter
13	bananas, beans, chocolate, sap, tires
14	gorillas, jaguars, nature
15	bats, blood, frog, predators, skin, snakes
16	lungs, planet
19	minute
20	fires

Check out www.av2books.com for activities, videos, audio clips, and more!

1 Go to www.av2books.com.

2 Enter book code. L 5 4 2 8 3 8

3 Fuel your imagination online!

www.av2books.com